THE MASSACRE AT DUN AN OIR 1580

Gearóid Ó Tuathaigh M.A.

Cló Dhuibhne, Ballyferriter, Tralee

Publishers: Cló Dhuibhne (a wholly owned subsidiary of Comharchumann Forbartha Chorca Dhuibhne), Ballyferriter, Tralee.

Contributions: Kerry County Library
The National Library of Ireland
Dingle Library
Public Record Office London (MPF 75)

ISBN 0 906096 04 9

First Edition 1980

Design: Mary McSweeney, Tralee

Printers: The Leinster Leader. Naas

Contents

Introduction _____ 1

Context _____ 2

Climax _____ 13

Epilogue _____ 27

Notes _____ 31

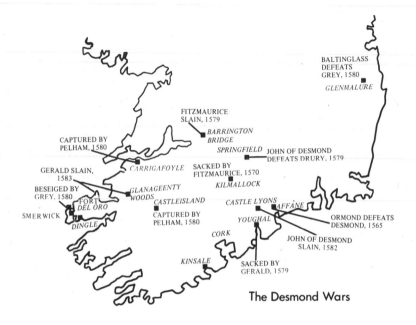

BALTINGLASS
DEFEATS
GREY, 1580
GLENMALURE

FITZMAURICE
SLAIN, 1579

BARRINGTON
BRIDGE

CAPTURED BY
PELHAM, 1580

SPRINGFIELD   JOHN OF DESMOND
DEFEATS DRURY, 1579

CARRIGAFOYLE   SACKED BY
FITZMAURICE, 1570

GERALD SLAIN,
1583

KILMALLOCK

BESEIGED BY
GREY, 1580   *GLANAGEENTY*
WOODS   *CASTLEISLAND*   CASTLE LYONS   *AFFANE*

FORT
DEL ORO   ORMOND DEFEATS
DESMOND, 1565

SMERWICK   CAPTURED BY   *YOUGHAL*
PELHAM, 1580

DINGLE   JOHN OF DESMOND
SLAIN, 1582

CORK

KINSALE   SACKED BY
GERALD, 1579

The Desmond Wars

Introduction

The Massacre at Dún an Óir, 1580

The sixteenth and seventeenth centuries saw many cruel and desperate deeds perpetrated as European **conquistadores** from different nations discovered and set about conquering new lands beyond the sea, particularly in the Americas. As the process of conquest and colonisation of the 'new world' gathered momentum many of the native peoples of the newly-discovered lands felt the edge of the swords of the new European masters. Whether these natives happened to be the Amerindians or the Gaelic Irish of Elizabethan times, the subjugation of 'barbarous peoples' and the establishment of 'civilized society' by the new conquerors was seldom achieved without much conflict and carnage. During these same centuries in Europe itself the wars of religion produced their own grim litany of atrocities, as cruel and horrific slaughter took place under the dual impulses of religious zeal and political ambition.[1] Yet, even by the standards of the age, the outrage which took place at Dún an Óir on 10 November 1580, when over five hundred men, Spanish, Italian and Irish, together with women and children, all unarmed, were massacred on the lonely fort, stands out as a particularly gruesome episode. F. M. Jones describes the massacre as *"one of the most ruthless episodes in the whole history of the Elizabethan wars in Ireland"*,[2] while Seán Ó Faoláin speaks of it as *"one of those incidents in history which though politically slight and unimportant in themselves will never be forgotten"*.[3] Certainly, the circumstances surrounding this tragic episode have been the source of disagreement and controversy from the very hour that the deed was done, and in recent times historians have sought to sift the surviving evidence and to reconstruct, without rancour, the story of the massacre at Dún an óir.[4] In this commemorative essay the object is to bring together the findings of these various historians. Before doing so, however, it is necessary to look at the general context, local and international, political, religious and military, in which the massacre took place.

1

Context

By the mid-sixteenth century the effective power of the central government in Ireland counted for little throughout wide areas of the country, when compared to the almost princely powers enjoyed by many of the Gaelic chiefs and by the main semi-feudal lords of Norman origin. Outside of the Pale, most of Ulster and north Connacht, parts of south-west Munster and south-east Leinster were under effective Gaelic control, while other parts of Leinster, most of Munster, together with counties Clare and Galway were the areas ruled by the great feudal lords. That the power of these mighty lords was not invincible had already been revealed in the eclipse of the mighty Kildare Geraldines during 1530s and 1540s, in the very early days of the assertion of Tudor power in Ireland. However, our concern here is with another branch of the Geraldines—the Desmonds—and with the later and more decisive phase of the Tudor conquest of Ireland under Elizabeth I. It was during the reign of the last of the Tudors that the entire island of Ireland finally came under the effective control of the crown and the central government, and that the almost independent local control of the great lords, Gaelic and Norman, was finally broken.

The defeat of the Munster Geraldines, in the course of which the Dún an Óir massacre was perpetrated, was an important chapter in the story of this crucial conquest of the local lords in Ireland by the Elizabethan government. But our canvas spreads wider even than the Elizabethan conquest of Ireland. The Desmond rebellion is part of the story of Catholic Europe in the age of the counter-reformation, a complex story with its centres of entreaty and intrigue in Rome, Paris and Madrid or along the Atlantic ports. In the matrix of religious conviction, political calculation and economic competition which constituted the great Anglo-Spanish rivalry of the later sixteenth century, the course of events in Ireland was of considerable importance. From the sixteenth century onwards Ireland's importance to a succession of European powers was based mainly on the calculation that Ireland could be used

Sir Henry Sidney

as a platform from which to strike at England. In short, in security terms Ireland was potentially England's Achilles heel. It was the tensions within Ireland, however,which produced the political instability and the opportunity required for a European intervention. Let us, therefore, take a closer look at these tensions.

When Elizabeth I succeeded to the English throne in 1558 there was already a growing consensus among some of the more influential royal advisors and administrators that the almost semi-feudal system of government and administration in Ireland, and particularly the almost unchecked local powers of the great lords, was an anachronism and ought to be ended. The powers of the local lords—in such areas as legal jurisdiction, the raising and quartering of private armies and the levying of taxes and other exactions—were increasingly seen as intolerable in an age when the nation-state was becoming more and more cohesive and centralized in its administration. The powers enjoyed by these great lords seemed incompatible with good and uniform administration, with a sensible and effective system of state revenue, or with the paramount issue of state security. From the mid-1560s, under the Deputyship of Sir Henry Sidney, there began a sustained attempt to change this situation, to impose a uniform system of law and administration throughout the country, and to curb and ultimately break the almost princely powers of the great lords. The evidence of this new drive can be seen in the renewal of the process of shiring, in the proceedings of Sidney's parliament of 1569-71, and in the establishment of provincial presidencies (with special military powers) in Munster and Connacht between 1569 and 1571. In the case of Sidney's parliament of 1569-71 the government gave clear notice of its intentions, by a series of proposals aimed at curbing the powers of the lords in such areas as raising and billeting private armies, and collecting revenue for themselves. The strength of the parliamentary opposition to these proposals (from the Anglo-Irish within and outside the Pale) showed that the government's new policy was perceived as being a serious threat to the existing power structures. The operation of the provincial presidencies—that is, the effective exercise of the powers and functions of the presidency—remained problematic (not least because of shortage of money) for some time after their establishment. But again they were portentous, a clear sign to the feudal lords that, if the government had its way, the days of their almost unchallenged local sway were numbered.

Two further factors combined to fan the smouldering discontent with the general thrust of government policy into open revolt in Munster. Firstly, there was the increasing influx of English Elizabethan adventurers into Munster from the 1560s onwards. As Dr. MacCurtain has written: ". . . the developing colonisation schemes in Elizabethan Ireland were attracting land-hungry adventurers and courtiers of varying background".[5] This encroachment of the new interlopers, and the complex political and legal intrigues which were often part and parcel of their attempts to secure land, was a further source of anxiety and unease to the local lords, adding a new dimension to their own rivalries and conflicting claims to title, tribute and jurisdiction. Some of these new adventurers had adroitly worked up claims to land based on long obsolete or entirely spurious Norman grants and titles, and for the local lords there was a disquietingly close association (on a personal and official level) between the land-hungry adventurers and the officials charged with implementing Sidney's political and administrative initiatives. These tendencies made even the greatest of the local lords restive; there was a growing feeling of insecurity about traditional powers, rights, functions and, now, even title to land.

Finally, there was the religious factor. Despite some early disquieting signs, no serious efforts had been made during the first decade of Elizabeth's reign to enforce the state religion or to make a sustained attack on the Irish Catholic interests. However, by the late 1560s the last faint hopes of a reconciliation between Elizabeth's England and Rome were dying fast, and in 1570 came the formal break with the papal bull of excommunication, **Regnans in excelsis.** This marked a crucial turning point. Henceforth Catholic resistance to the Elizabethan

Queen Elizabeth I

5

state could be couched in religious terms, as a repudiation of the authority of an heretic. In short, a rebellion could become a crusade. On the other hand, the final break with Rome meant for Elizabeth and her commanders that Catholics within the realm were now, whatever protests of loyalty they might make, not to be trusted. This new development in the religious sphere was an important element in the gathering crisis in Ireland, and particularly in Munster.

Of all the feudal lords, none was likely to find the new intrusive threat of government policy more unwelcome than the Earl of Desmond. There were several reasons why this should be so. In the first place, as Dr. Canny has noted, *"the earl of Desmond represented the independence of the feudal lords in its most aggressive form"*.[6] Since 1468 the earls of Desmond had *"only sporadic contact with Dublin, and ruled as almost independent princes over counties Kerry, Limerick, Waterford and north Cork. Much of the Desmonian power had been lost by the mid-sixteenth century, but Earl Gerald still held courts at Tralee and Any,had almost absolute control of north Kerry and Limerick, and, as late as 1568, denied the queen's sheriff the right to arrest any member of the Fitzgerald family since 'he taketh that he ought to be ther judg' "*.[7] It was almost inevitable that one who enjoyed such wide powers by tradition should find the new policies of Sidney hard to take. There were complicating factors, however. For one thing Gerald, the fourteenth Earl of Desmond (who had succeeded to the title in 1558), was a rather weak and indecisive man, physically unprepossessing and lacking in political shrewdness. His main problems in the early years after his succession lay in settling innumerable border disputes with the traditional great rivals of the Munster Geraldines, the Earls of Ormond. Here the 14th Earl of Desmond was unfortunate, in that he was a contemporary of Black Tom Butler, the 10th earl of Ormond, a man who had been educated in the inner circle of the court and who, throughout Elizabeth's reign, remained the royal favourite and the trusted party in any disputes between Ormond and Desmond. Already in the early 1560s Desmond had been summoned to London because of the state of almost open war which existed between himself and Ormond. Now in 1567 both Earls, who were again in a state of war, were summoned to London to explain themselves. Desmond was to be detained in London, to all intents and purposes under house arrest, for the best part of six years. Much was to happen during that fateful interval of the Earl's absence.

In 1569 there began a series of revolts, during the course of which, at various times during the next six years, branches of the foremost feudal lordships—Desmond, Ormond, Thomond and Clanricard—as well as many lesser lords and Gaelic chieftains, struck out at the new colonizers

6

and adventurers and at the new system of government and those who were judged to be supporters of it. The revolts were, for the most part, highly local; they all involved the settling of local scores in summary and brutal fashion; they were largely conservative in purpose, in that they sought to protect existing powers against the encroachments of the new system. In all cases, however, the 'rebels' were either defeated or else forced to make terms which effectively accepted the thrust of the government's new policies. The one major exception to this pattern of local 'rearguard-action' revolts was that led by James Fitzmaurice Fitzgerald, a cousin of the exiled Earl of Desmond.

The lengthy detention of the Earl in London (and the arrest in 1568 of his brother, Sir John of Desmond), created a power vacuum within the Desmond lordship. This vacuum was filled by James Fitzmaurice Fitzgerald who was, in every important respect, of very different mettle indeed to the exiled earl. A dashing soldier, a decisive and daring opportunist, an ambitious man (who saw his chance to effectively 'take over' the vacant earldom while the seniors of the house were absent, with no certainty of their return), Fitzmaurice was, furthermore, a zealous Catholic of strong religious convictions, and was fully in tune with the political dimension of counter-reformation Catholicism in Europe. When, ironically, a bloody and bitter general quarrel between Sir Edmund Butler (a brother of Black Tom) and Sir Peter Carew (one of the more unscrupulous of the adventurers) triggered off a series of revolts by the feudal lords in defence of their powers, Fitzmaurice seized his opportunity. However, even though he too had personal ambitions, Fitzmaurice went beyond the essentially local demands of the other lords, by calling on Catholic Ireland to join him in a holy war against the 'heretic' English. Fitzmaurice showed considerable courage, daring and resourcefulness in his efforts to increase the momentum of the revolt. Symbolically donning Gaelic dress he recruited to his banner many of the Gaelic chieftains of the south-west—McCarthy Mór, McDonagh, O'Keeffe, O'Sullivan Mór and O'Sullivan Beare. On the international front, Fitzmaurice had the papal appointee to the archbishopric of Cashel, Maurice Fitzgibbon, scheming and sueing at the court of Philip II in an attempt to get assistance for the Catholic 'crusade' in Munster. Fitzmaurice wasted no time in showing that he meant business. The seats of the St. Legers and the Grenvilles were attacked; at different times between 1569 and 1573 Cork, Youghal and Kinsale were threatened. In his most spectacular act of aggression Fitzmaurice burned Kilmallock. However, though he might enjoy occasional successes, Fitzmaurice's holy war eventually ended in failure. Foreign aid did not arrive. The other feudal lords were only interested in their local power base and, one by one, beginning with the

Butlers after the return of the crafty Black Tom to Ormond in 1569, they made terms and promised loyalty to the government. The Lord Deputy, Sir Henry Sidney, moved south in the summer of 1569, and with a force which eventually exceeded a thousand he gradually cowed the opposition by a greater show of force. The Butlers were now co-operating with the government for the rest of Elizabeth's reign. Gradually Fitzmaurice's allies began to disengage and to make terms. However, submission did not bring immunity. When Humphrey Gilbert (one of the much-resented adventurers) was given the title of colonel and the task of 'pacifying' Munster he did so *"with a new ruthlessness that made death the wages of revolt"*.[8] The hard-line pacification was continued under Sir John Perrot, the tough lord President of Munster between 1571 and 1573. And, although Fitzmaurice rallied bravely from time to time and found temporary shelter in the Glen of Aherlow his ultimate submission was inevitable. It came in February 1573 when Fitzmaurice finally submitted unconditionally to Perrot, whereupon Fitzmaurice and his followers were forced to *"yelde themselves in certeyne good townes with halters about their necks, and such lyke punnishment for terrors sake"*.[9]

The final collapse of Fitzmaurice's revolt coincided with the return of the Earl of Desmond to his ancestral lands. As a conciliatory gesture (and contrary to Perrot's advice) the earl was permitted to return to Ireland in 1573 on the strict conditions that he would keep the peace, accept the reformed church and make no attempt to extend his power or jurisdiction at the expense of his neighbours. On his return the Earl spent several months in Dublin virtually in a state of detention, but he eventually made his way south, was ensconced in his castle in Askeaton before the end of the year, and, was showing signs (such as the wearing of the prohibited Gaelic dress) that he was about to resume the life of semi-feudal grandeur which he aspired to. He soon found out, however, that under the new regime there was no question of a resumption of 'business as usual' after the old fashion. In the summer of 1574 the combined forces of the Lord Deputy, Fitzwilliam, and of Ormond executed the garrison of one of Desmond's castles, in a sharp lesson to him that any attempt to renege on his promises or to revert to the 'old ways' would not be tolerated. Thereafter the Earl's main concern was with survival. He wanted to enjoy as many of his traditional rights and powers as possible while, at the same time, doing nothing to arouse the suspicion or the anger of the government. It was

8

a difficult game to play. Desmond knew that the Queen and her closest advisors disliked him and that his arch-rival Ormond lost no opportunity to blacken his name in court circles. But his long detention in London had taught him to be wary.

During Desmond's detention in England, he wrote several letters protesting his loyalty, and of one of these, by the kindness of Mr. A. Fitzgibbon, we are here enabled to submit to the Association a fac-simile executed by Netherclift of London. The letter reads as follows:-

"In most humbliest wise my duetie to your honourable estates remembrid, For as moch as I vnderstand that swete is made by my Brother, Sr John, to haue a chardge into the west partes of Ireland for the suppression of the rebelles ther, the whiche if it should come to passe would geve me an occasion to thinke that your honnours do either suspect my trewe and loyall seruice towards my soveraigne Lady the Quene, or els do judge me vnhable to geve them the overthrowe, whiche besedes that they are traytours to her Matie so haue they bene vtter enemyse and spoylers of all my patrymony. For answere whereof and especially for my good mynd towardes the Quenes ma^{tie}, God who knoweth the secrettes of all mens harts *save me or els dampne me as my hart* is well bent towardes her hignes, besedes the which I haue offred good Suerties for the good performans of my duetie hereafter and that for *the obtainynge of my Libertie into* my contrey, whereby I do not doubt but like as I am best hable, so in shortest tyme, and that with lesse chardge to her ma^{tie} I should bothe quiette the contrey *and bring the rebelles to utter confusion*. These are therefore humbly to requeste your honours to stand so good vnto me as to be a meane to her ma^{tie} to grant me the prefermente of the matter before any other. Wherin I shall thinke myself most bound vnto her hignes in *wouchsafing to repose so greate a truste in me, and here withall* I do promisse so to behave myself therein as that her ma^{tie} shall hereafter haue good cause to thinke well of my seruices, and thus eftsones requesting your honours to stand good unto me I humbly take my leave, from Sentleger House the xxth of August 1571.
"Your honours most bounden,
"GEROT DESMOND.

"To the right honorable
the Quenes ma^{ties}'most honourable
privie Counsell."

Transcript of Desmond's Letter

9

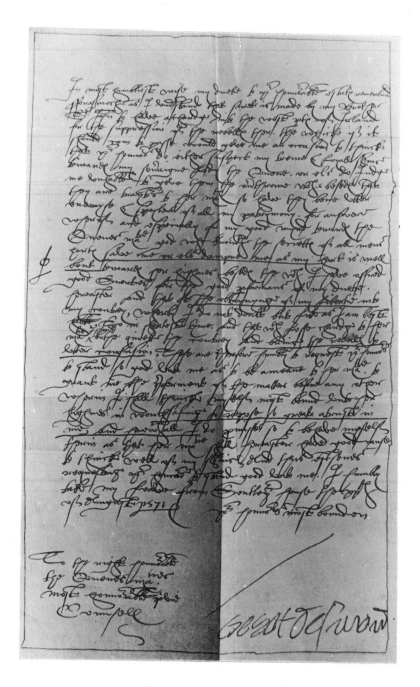

Letter from Garóid Earl of Desmond

10

Though not a very zealous man in religious matters, he was, nevertheless, a loyal Catholic; and he found the religious no less than the political and administrative aspects of the new policy repugnant to him. Given the thrust of government policy it was probably inevitable that Desmond would eventually have to chose between accepting a major and permanent reduction of his traditional rights and powers, or open resistance to the new policies. Determined as the earl was to postpone for as long as possible the day of choice, two major factors combined to force his hand. In the first place, the government was determined to press ahead with its assault on the powers of the feudal lords in Munster. In particular, Sir William Drury, as President of Munster during 1576-8, was untiring in his suppression of private armies, 'masterless men', and in his efforts to regularize and maximize the revenue collected for the central government. Drury's regime was one of considerable violence. Hundreds were executed, many of them tried under martial law. Desmond, no less than the other Munster lords, became restive and alarmed at the implementation of state policy by Drury in Munster. But it was the activities of the Earl's cousin, the ubiquitous James Fitzmaurice Fitzgerald, which set alight this smouldering keg of discontent in Munster and which finally drew the Earl into open rebellion against the crown.

Following his defeat in 1573 Fitzmaurice spent almost two unhappy years watching the growing menace of the government's policies force the Earl into one humiliating submission after another in his battle for survival. In the case of Fitzmaurice, his own ambitions had been disappointed; his pride as a Geraldine was hurt by the sight of his cousin's weak and (as Fitzmaurice saw it) timid struggle for survival;his religious convictions were outraged by the attempt to call for adherence to the reformed church after Elizabeth's excommunication in 1570. Unable to do much to change the situation at home, Fitzmaurice was one, and the most illustrious one, of a group of clerics, noblemen and soldiers—many of them Irish exiles—who shuffled to and from between the capitals of Catholic Europe in an attempt to enlist the aid of the Catholic rulers for a major intervention in Ireland as part of a counter-reformation strategy against Protestant England.

In France, Fitzmaurice and his fellow emissaries found fair words of encouragement, but no aid. Likewise in Spain, though they found sympathy with their cause (on religious and strategic grounds) at the court of Philip II, nevertheless here also raison d'état was the paramount consideration. Absorbed in his struggle in the Netherlands, and watchful of developments in neighbouring France, Philip II was not yet prepared for an open confrontation with England. The Irish would have to be patient. In the event, it was the Papacy, in the person of

An Irish Feast

Pope Gregory XIII, which came forward with practical aid for the Irish. At first, however, Papal aid was bestowed on a most unlikely recipient, one Thomas Stukeley, an English adventurer who, disappointed in his hopes of advancement in the crown service in Ireland, had also been plying the Pope and Philip II with optimistic forecasts of what he could achieve for the Catholic cause in ireland if only he could raise an army. Stukeley was not trusted by some of the Irish exiles in Europe. Nevertheless, in 1578 the Pope *"provided Stukeley with a ship, six hundred* **condottieri,** *a hundred thousand ducats, and a monthly allowance of another thousand . . ."*.[10] Stukeley set sail from Rome with his expeditionary force in Spring 1578; his rotten boat needed to be replaced at Lisbon. As it happened, however, Stukeley instead of continuing to Ireland now joined the King of Portugal in an expedition to north Africa, where he was killed in battle with the Moors in August 1578. It seemed as if the Papal expedition to Ireland had been totally aborted. The Pope and James Fitzmaurice Fitzgerald were determined, however, that this should not be the end of the enterprise, and while the most vigorous Papal promptings failed to persuade Philip II to give open support to an Irish expedition, Fitzmaurice was allowed to recruit a force of 'volunteers' round Ferrol. Eventually he succeeded in recruiting about eighty Spaniards, a small number of Italians and a mixed group of Irish and English Catholic exiles. In military terms it was a rather poor force, whether the yardstick is one of quantity or quality. Nevertheless, with this force Fitzmaurice, carrying with him the Papal Legate, Dr. Nicholas Sanders, set sail in six ships from Santander on 17 June, 1579 to begin his holy war of liberation in Ireland.

Climax

Fitzmaurice reached the Kerry coast in early July, 1579. The force did not land at Dingle as originally intended. Bad weather intervened however, and scattered the ships. A small force landed in Dingle and discovered that hostile pro-government elements had been alerted to their impending arrival and consequently no welcome awaited them there. Sailing round to Árd na Caithne bay the force disembarked there at the fort of Dún an Óir, which had been built the previous year by one Peter Rice, ostensibly to attract visitors interested in fishing, but, according to suspicious government sources, in reality in preparation for Fitzmaurice's landing. Undismayed by the small size of his force,[11] Fitzmaurice promptly unfurled the Papal banner and called on the Catholic nobles to do their duty by their religion, and to rise against the government. There were early signs of encouragement; from Galway the O'Malleys and the O'Flahertys sent ships to assess the seriousness of Fitzmaurice's challenge. Dr. Sanders, an iron-willed champion of the counter-reformation and a former professor of theology at Louvain, kept in touch with Rome, calling for more aid, while at the same time calling on the Irish Catholics to be steadfast to their faith and to join with Fitzmaurice. Unfortunately, however, Fitzmaurice himself was not destined to remain at the head of the Papal army for very long. In an attempt to spread the revolt throughout Munster, Fitzmaurice moved north into Limerick on his way (in pilgrimage) to Holycross in Tipperary, and with the clear intention of raising rebellion in those counties. He faced opposition, however, from some of the local families, and in a skirmish with the Limerick Burkes on 18 August 1579 Fitzmaurice met his death at Béal Átha an Bhóithrín, about two miles north-west of Cappamore, co. Limerick. His death removed from the rebellion its most colourful and, arguably, its most formidable political figure.

One of the main reasons which had forced Fitzmaurice to move north in an attempt to extend the rebellion to Tipperary and Limerick was the early response of the Earl of Desmond to the arrival of the Papal force.

The Cittie or Burrough Bay of Tripoli

The three Cisters

Admiral Winter's Map of Smerwick

Siege of 1580—the work is attributed to Admiral Winter himself

The original can be seen in the Public Records Office, London and is very attractive (in colour) — M.P.F. 75

Despite passionate appeals (couched in strong moral terms) from Fitzmaurice, the Earl showed no early desire to become involved in the rebellion. In fact the Earl and his wife were at great pains to keep their options open by, on the one hand, communicating with the government and denying any knowledge or support of the rebellion, while on the other hand taking care not to repudiate his kinsman and the papal banner openly. Even after his brothers, John and James, had both joined the rebellion, the tormented Earl still tried to keep his balance on the fence. He eventually found, however, that there could be no neutral ground in this kind of struggle. The government's profound mistrust of him—constantly fuelled by his great rival, Ormond—meant that the only way he could unequivocally show his loyalty was by himself taking the field against his brothers and the papal army. This the Earl simply could not do without rendering meaningless his own position as head of the Munster Geraldines. Inch by inch, the Earl was pushed into taking sides, until finally,'and with a weary heart, he joined the rebels in October 1579. On 2 November 1579 he was formally proclaimed a traitor by the Lord Justice, Sir William Pelham. Seán Ó Faoláin's dramatic version of the Earl's finally throwing in his lot with the rebels owes much to a vivid literary imagination; but, in essence, it is also remarkably close to the historical truth:

> ". . . Desmond found himself edged into revolt. The standard of a religious crusade in which he hardly believed was placed in his palsied hands. He was lifted to his horse. The kernes shouted the war cry before him, *Pápa Abú,* and all Catholic Munster rose behind him. By January 1580 though now to the English 'this mad-brained Earl, the only arch-traitor in all Ireland', he had become the focal point of the entire secret Catholic league in Europe . . . His role was tremendous. If he had only been equal to the occasion he might have hammered himself into a great symbol. Poor, racked, doubting man, he was the most improbable, leaking vessel that ever held a precious idea . . .".[12]

In one sense, the Earl's joining the rebels made the government's task in dealing with the rebellion less complicated. It could now use total repression throughout the province, with the gloves off. And this, in effect, was what happened. Already in late summer Sir William Drury (Lord Justice in Dublin after Sidney's resignation in 1578) had moved in strength to crush the rebellion. On Drury's death in September 1579, Sir Nicholas Malby (who had been a 'hard-line' governor of Connacht) was appointed temporary governor of Munster; Sir William Pelham became Lord Justice; and the Earl of Ormond became general of Munster. Together these three determined to put down the revolt in

16

Phillip II of Spain

Munster, with the strongest arm possible. In effect a reign of terror and destruction was instituted, where summary executions of suspected rebels took place daily and where wide areas of good land were laid waste in punitive drives across Munster. Not surprisingly, the Desmond lands in particular were ravaged, with an almost perverse satisfaction, by the Earl of Ormond. Pelham in his despatches was quite explicit in explaining the purpose of this scorched earth policy. On 27 July 1580 Pelham wrote to the Queen that, *"the harvest being now come, I purpose to destroy their corn, the fear where of has made many of them to seek protections and pardons, and bred contentions between the Earl and his followers."*[13] And a fortnight later (on 12 August) he added further details of his strategy to isolate the Earl:

> *"Touching my manner of prosecuting, it is thus: I give the rebels no breath to relieve themselves, but by one of your garrisons or other they be continually hunted. I keep them from their harvest, and have taken great preys of cattle from them, by which it seemeth the poor people that lived only upon labour, and fed by their milch cows, are so distressed, as they follow their goods and offer themselves with their wives and children rather to be slain by the army than to suffer the famine that now in extremity beginneth to pinch them".*[14]

17

It will be clear from these excerpts that by the summer of 1580 the government forces were very decidedly on the offensive against the rebels throughout Munster. It is true that the Earl of Desmond, when he eventually joined the rebellion, had begun with a flourish, capturing and sacking Youghal (where he had the royal arms pulled from the courthouse and trampled underfoot); threatening Cork, and meting out sudden and harsh punishment to government (particularly Ormond) sympathisers, and indeed to those of his own clients whose loyalty was suspect. However, by Spring 1580 the initiative had clearly passed to the stronger government forces. With Pelham and Ormond in charge of the land forces and Sir William Winter in charge on sea, the royal forces systematically combed Desmond's lands, executing at will, pillaging, driving off cattle and burning the crops. Desmond's fort at Carrigfoyle was taken and the entire garrison executed, and counties Kerry and Limerick were subjected to massive occupation and reprisal by the government forces. Desmond abandoned his castles and took to the woods and hills with his followers. One by one his Munster allies were forced to submit—the McCarthys, O'Sullivans, O'Callaghans and McDonaghs. Fitzmaurice's fond hope (still cherished by Dr. Sanders, by now inseparable from Desmond's forces) that Catholic Ireland would rally to the Papal standard, was not realized. Apart from a few local distrubances west of the Shannon, the only serious, positive response to Fitzmaurice's call for a Catholic league came in Spring 1980 in faraway Wicklow, with a rising led by James Eustace, the Viscount Baltinglass. This was insufficient, however, to seriously alter the situation in Munster. As Dr. Sanders and others continually emphasised in desperate and exasperated letters to the Pope and to Philip II, only a major expeditionary force (of the order of 8,000 men, well-victualled) could now turn the tide in Munster. Sadly, when a second expedition eventually set sail from Santander on 28 August 1580 it fell far short, both in numbers and in quality, of the minimum force requested by Sanders and the rebels.

The force, which probably numbered about seven to eight hundred men when it set sail, was comprised of Spaniards (mostly from the Basque region),[15] Italians and a small number of others, mostly Irish exiles. It was led by an Italian, Sebastiano di San Giuseppe, a man seriously deficient in courage, competence and, as it transpired, honour. The force, sailing in six vessels, reached the Kerry coast in mid-September; some ships became separated because of bad weather; and, having decided against putting in at Dingle, San Giuseppe finally weighed anchor in Árd na Caithne bay and put ashore at Dún an Óir. The force was not a very experienced one, but it was well-armed and well-victualled, having carried arms and supplies for the expected local force with which it was to join. Lord Grey afterwards reported that:

> There was found in the forts good store of money, and a great quantity of biscuits, bacon, oil, fish, rice, beans, peas, barley, being by computation victuals for their company for half a year. There was also found armour, murrions, calivers, muskets, pikes, swords, flasks,harquebusses of croke, powder, shot, barrels of bullets, and other kind of furniture, to serve 3,000 men, and sundry tools for men of all occupations".[16]

Having disembarked,[17] San Giuseppe's force set to strengthening the fort at Dún an Óir. It seems that they had difficulty collecting wood, due to a scarcity of wood in the immediate vicinity, and also, according to San Giuseppe, because local contacts refused to provide them with a sufficient supply of timber. The fort itself was built on "a small spur of land jutting into Smerwick Harbour",[18] and it was estimated to be no more than forty feet by twenty feet in size. However, the garrison was not quite so cramped as this would suggest, since an eighteen foot high rampart had been constructed enclosing some of the land adjoining the promontory. San Giuseppe seems to have considered the fort a good, defensible base. Writing to Rome on 1 October 1580 he stated:

> "at the moment I am engaged in fortifying my position in a spot called 'il Castel dell'Oro' where with a few soldiers we shall easily be able to guard the war supplied from any attack by the enemy."[19]

However,the general opinion of the fort, both then and since, was that it was a very poor position for the garrison. Sir Nicholas White, who visited the fort (with Pelham's force) in summer 1580 recorded that the fort was "judged by men of skyll a place of noe strength".[20] Shortly after the massacre the Spanish ambassador in London informed Philip II that "The Queen is informed that it would have been impossible to have found a worse place to build a fort, since it neither commanded a port nor a land pass, had no natural capabilities for defence and did not even possess in the neighbourhood wood for fuel".[21] Finally, there is Sir Charles Petrie's recent verdict that: "This fort is overlooked in every direction, so it is not surprising that what should have been a bridge-head became a death-trap".[22]

It was probably these considerations, among others, which prompted local leaders to urge the expeditionary force to leave the fort and to fan out (as Fitzmaurice's 1579 force had done) throughout the countryside. However, after a few brief sorties outside, the expeditionary force elected instead to opt for what turned out to be the cruelly deceptive 'safety' of the fort.

Apart from a few minor skirmishes, the most notable incident in the few weeks immediately following the landing was the arrival of Ormond and his forces outside the fort.

However, Ormond was not equipped for a siege, and so he withdrew to Rathkeale to await reinforcements. By late October this main royal army, led by the new Lord Deputy, Lord Grey de Wilton, was fast approaching the Dingle peninsula. Lord Grey, a stern and ruthless puritan with a stomach for unpleasant assignments (he was subsequently one of the commissioners for the trial of Mary, Queen of Scots) had only been a short time in the country, having been appointed Lord Deputy in August 1580. He had, however, been long enough installed for his forces to have suffered a surprise and humiliating defeat in an ambush in Glenmalure while pursuing the Wicklow rebels. Not surprisingly, Grey was anxious to expunge the bitter memory of this early reverse, and he moved with speed and resolution to challenge the invading force at the earliest possible opportunity, before it could consolidate its position or link up with what remained of Desmond's scattered forces in Munster, to act as a platform for a renewal of the rebellion. Grey's own force probably numbered about eight hundred, but it linked with Ormond's force on land and was also joined by Admiral Winter's fleet which effectively blockaded Árd na Caithne bay. On 7 November 1580 the siege of Dún an Óir began. The royal army included many of the best known of the Elizabethan captains in Ireland—Zouch, Raleigh, Macworth, Achen, Bingham and others, including the poet Spenser (as Grey's secretary), and the young baron of Dungannon.[23] It is not certain what was the exact number within the fort on 7 November. It is possible that some of the expeditionary force (about 200 of them) may have returned to Europe before early November. On the other hand SanGiuseppe's force was probably augmented by some of Fitzmaurice's 1579 force returning to Dún an Óir to join the newcomers. Furthermore, it must be remembered that there were also in the fort a number of women and children who, no doubt, in expectation of hostilities and reprisals, had sought refuge in the fort. In all, it seems plausible to suggest a figure of about 600 for the garrison of the fort when the siege began.[24]

Following slight skirmishes on the 7th the firing became heavier during the 8th, and the main casualty on the government side was one, John Cheke, a nephew of Lord Burghley. The response of the garrison in Dún an Óir to Grey's bombardment deserves brief mention. On the 8th, it seems, two flags were hoisted above the fort—a white and a black flag—in place of the papal flag and four ensigns which had so provoked Grey upon his arrival at the fort. It was subsequently claimed by San Giuseppe that these white and black flags were an agreed signal to Desmond's forces to come to the aid of the garrison. No such aid arrived, however, and when the right flank of the fort was effectively demolished by bombardment San Giuseppe took down the

20

black flag on the 9th leaving a white flag indicating a wish to negotiate. Talks between the two sides began on the 9th. It is on this part of the story that the cloud of controversy and recrimination has settled most firmly. This is not surprising. The various accounts of what transpired during these negotiations are full of contradictions and inconsistencies. It is impossible to give an absolutely accurate account of the talks between Grey and San Giuseppe, the most vital part of the negotiations.

However, notwithstanding these difficulties in assessing the evidence, it is possible to sketch the course of events and to suggest the most probable explanations of what happened.

The first parley was conducted by, on Grey's side, Captain Wingfield (Master of the Ordnance) and it seems, by Alessandro Bertoni (the campmaster) on behalf of the garrison. Bertoni had as his interpreter one Oliver Plunkett, an Irishman from near Drogheda.[25] Plunkett was one of three victims in the fort whose fate was to be particularly cruel. The other two were an English servant of Dr. Sanders, whose name was variously given as William Woolich or Woolish or Walsh,and a priest named Laurence Moore. These three were taken prisoners before the massacre, and when, after a lengthy interrogation, they refused to renounce their religion, they were tortured. It seems they were taken to a forge[26] where their limbs were broken; they were subsequently hanged and their bodies hung as targets on which the soldiers could practice.

At any rate, Plunkett was Bertoni's interpreter. Grey was not satisfied to parley with Bertoni and wanted to have talks with a Spaniard (the international context would have made this a sensible demand). After some further talks, during which the garrison released a hostage, Sir James Fitzgarrett of the Decies, as an earnest of good faith, San Giuseppe himself finally came to negotiate with Grey. At this stage it is worth adverting to the state of morale within the fort, and to the object of San Giuseppe's negotiations.

It is clear that San Giuseppe, contrary to his own account, was not anxious to continue the fight and was anxious to make such terms with Grey as would, at the very least, save his own skin. He was probably one of the strongest advocates of surrender. His advice was contested within the fort, most vigorously by Ercole Pisano, some other officers and by Plunkett and Fr. Moore. Those advocating resistance based their arguments on two main considerations; firstly, that honour and the cause they served demanded that they make a fight of it (especially as they were well-armed); and, secondly, that they should fight at least long enough to allow Desmond's forces to close in on Grey's forces from the land side.

21

It was during San Giuseppe's talks with Grey that Plunkett was suspected of deliberately misinterpreting the statements of both parties, with a view to frustrating San Giuseppe's proposed surrender. As soon as his suspicions were aroused San Giuseppe became angry with Plunkett, had him arrested, and afterwards handed him over (together with Fr. Moore and Mr. Wollich) as Grey's prisoners. So far as the terms of surrender are concerned, Grey's account stated unequivocally that no terms were offered by him to San Giuseppe, that he called for an unconditional surrender, that all arms should be surrendered and that it be left entirely to Grey's discretion whether or not to grant mercy. The precise standing of the garrison (within the rules of war) was somewhat difficult. They were not soldiers of the king of Spain—after all Spain and England were not at war. They were, in fact, soldiers of the Pope, and when Bertoni admitted to Grey that they had been sent by the Pope *"for the defence of the Catholica Fede"*, Grey left him in no doubt about his attitude towards Rome:

> *"I would not greatly have marvelled if men being commanded by natural and absolute Princes did sometimes taken in hand wrong action; but that men—and that of account as some of them made show of _ should have been carried into unjust, desperate and wicked actions by one that neither from God nor man could claim any princely power or empire—but indeed a detestable shaveling, the right Antichrist and general ambitions tyrant over all right principalities and patron of the diabolica fede—I could not but greatly rest in wonder; their fault therefore for to be aggravated by the vileness of their commander; and that at any hands no condition of composition they were to expect other than that they should render me the Fort and yield their selves to my will for life or death".*[27]

Notwithstanding these strong words (which, after all, were meant to gratify his Queen) there persists the belief in the Spanish, Roman and Irish sources that Grey eventually offered terms to San Giuseppe; that in order to secure the immediate surrender of the fort Grey promised a free passage and departure out of Ireland to the garrison. We have no way of giving a definitive answer to this problem. What seems incontrovertible, however, is that San Giuseppe led the garrison to believe that terms had been agreed which would allow them safe passage out of the fort, and ultimately, home. It is likely that this was the main concern of the majority of the garrison at this stage; whatever appetite these relatively raw recruits may have had for fighting was well and truly gone by 10 November. At any rate it seems clear that it was

22

on the understanding (given to them by San Giuseppe) that they would be given a safe exit that they surrendered their arms and allowed the fort to be occupied.

Sir Walter Raleigh

On the morning of the 10th San Giuseppe and ten or twelve others came from the fort and surrendered their ensigns to Grey, who promptly sent in soldiers to gather up the surrendered arms and ammunition and to guard the victuals. The fort and the fate of its garrison were now in Grey's hands.

What happened next is not in dispute. A massacre began, or, to quote Grey himself: *"Then put I in certain bands who straight fell to execution. There were six hundred slain".*[28] All the Irish men and women were hanged (probably to the number of twenty); the Italians and Spaniards were executed; all except fifteen hand-picked survivors who, with San Giuseppe, had been taken into protective custody before the massacre began. The bodies of the executed were probably pushed over the cliff into the sea, and references by later commentators to bodies being laid out on beaches can only refer to bodies being subsequently washed up on the beaches of the peninsula.

The torture and execution of the three prisoners—Plunkett, Moore and Wollich(?)—has already been noted. Let us now look at the fifteen who escaped. It is quite clear that special terms were made for them by San Giuseppe. But it is equally clear that neither nationality nor rank were used as criteria in the selection of these fortunate survivors. There were Spaniards and Italians among the survivors, and the fifteen comprised one colonel, two captains, one campmaster, one friar, one notary apostolic, one ensignbearer, one sergeant, one corporal, and six privates.If, as San Giuseppe claimed, the 'prisoners' were held for ransom then it is rather strange that the profit motive was so conspicuously neglected—the ransoms varied from 4,000 to 120 scudi.[29] What emerges as the most likely explanation to this episode is that San Giuseppe probably got a guarantee of clemency for a number of his own cronies and that he either surrendered the remainder of the garrison in the uncertain hope that Grey would grant them mercy or else that he abandoned them knowing full well what their fate would be. In either case his conduct was dishonourable. The tradition which makes 'Grey's faith' synonymous with treachery may be based on nothing more than Grey's connivance at San Giuseppe's deception of his own men, or it may be based on something more culpable. But San Giuseppe's treachery towards his own comrades-in-arms seems undeniable and inexcusable.

So far as those who actually perpetrated the massacre are concerned, the sources are divided on the question of whether it was Edmund Denny or Sir Walter Raleigh who actually commanded the group which carried out the execution. Again, local tradition leans to the view that Raleigh was the main culprit, and the use of Raleigh's name to quieten or frighten children is revealing evidence of the impression left by Raleigh's deeds on the popular imagination.[30] The notion that Grey's act was an isolated act of personal cruelty, frowned on by his superiors and particularly by the Queen, can not be seriously maintained. Grey himself wrote a lengthy account of the massacre (omitting very few details) to Elizabeth. The religious fanaticism which sustained him in his righteous defence of such a monstrous act is clearly revealed in the letter already quoted in this essay.[31] More revealing still, however, is the Queen's response to Grey's account, a response which deserves to be quoted at some length:

> "As the most happy success you have lately had against certain invaders sent by the Pope, contained in your letters brought unto us by our servant Denny doth incomparably show the greatness of God's love and favour towards us; so your care and pain in following of the same and courage in execution thereof deserveth great thanks and commendations at our hands. Wherein you have answered by effects the good opinion we conceived of your sufficiency at the time of our choice made of you to supply the place you do now hold: not doubting but that hereafter there will appear greater fruits of your valour by reducing the distressed state of the realm to such conformity as God may be better served, we obeyed and this our realm not burdened with charges as of late years it has been.'Wherein assure yourself you shall not lack our good countenance and favour in such measure as neither enny nor practice shall be able to prevail against you; and therefore with this assurance you may proceed with the more comfort in the charge committed unto you.'
>
> In this late enterprise performed by you so greatly to our liking, we could have wished that the principal persons of the said invaders to whom you have promised grace, which we will see performed, had been reserved for us, to have extended towards them either justice or merce as to us should have been found best. For that it seems to us more agreeable to reason that a principal should receive punishment before an accessory: which would have served for a terror to such as may be hereafter drawn to be executioners of so wicked an enterprise, when they should here that as well the heads as the inferiors had received punishment according to their demerits".[32]

The only words of regret here are, significantly, on the score of Grey's having taken upon himself the discretionary power of clemency and having given the prisoners to some of his captains in order to raise ransom. The deed itself is applauded. The serious business of conquest was not for the squeamish, and Elizabeth no less than Grey realised this. Those who were most prominent in the massacre were well rewarded for their loyalty and zeal. For example, Edmund Denny was given Tralee and a tidy seignory in Kerry as a reward for his exertions. As for the prisoners held 'for ransom', it seems that some of them at least were held for a time at a castle at Waltham in Essex, but "under such lax guard" that they could escape without much difficulty. Eventually in 1583 the prisoners, including San Giuseppe, finally made their escape. Others had already paid dearly for the freedom of San Giuseppe and his associates.

It remains only to ask how exceptional or unique was this maccacre at Dún an Óir? Certainly, as we noted in the preface, historians are agreed that it was one of the most horrific acts of a bloody era. We must, however, set the episode in context. In fact gruesome massacres —of unarmed men, women and children—were already well-established in the Elizabethan conquest of Ireland before 1580. For example, it was only six years before Dún an Óir that Essex had massacred the population of Rathlin island. The Desmond wars in Munster from the late sixties had produced a long litany of cruel and savage acts. The conquest of the Amerindians and the excesses of the wars of religion in Europe are stories with more than their quota of wanton cruelty and the spilling of innocent blood. Yet for all that, Grey's cold-blooded execution of an unarmed garrison who had surrendered in expectation that their lives would be spared, remains an act of grave iniquity. That it was so perceived by contemporaries and by later generations is clearly evidenced in the remarkable shame and abhorrence which attaches to Grey's name and to his deed in the folk tradition of Kerry to this very day.

Epilogue

The aftermath of the Dún an Óir massacre need not detain us long. It is a tragic story of destruction and slaughter. In Leinster Fiach MacHugh held out until he received satisfactory terms. Lord Baltinglass fled to Spain. The Desmond castles fell, one by one, to the English forces. Youghal, Carrigfoyle, Askeaton and Ballylogh were surrendered. The Earl's brothers both met their deaths; James, having been captured in a raid, was hanged and quartered in Cork and his head placed on a spike near one of the city gates for months; John was murdered by a former servant. The Earl of Desmond, and all who were suspected of being in any sympathy with him, were hunted down and "stalked like vermin".[33] A policy of systematic destruction and terror was undertaken, to punish Munster and to teach a lesson. The rich lands of Munster were laid to waste, so that the Four Masters could record that *"the lowing of a cow or a voice of a ploughman could scarcely be heard from Dún Chaoin to Cashel . . ."*[34] The tragic Earl, moving Lear-like from cave to cave, seeking the shelter of wood and mountain with an ever-diminishing band of faithful followers,managed to evade his pursuers until the bleak winter of 1583. By this time *"his people were so much in dread and awe of the law and sovereign of England that they began to separate from him, even his own married wife, children and friends, so that he had but four persons to accompany him from one cavern of a rock or hollow of a tree to another . . ."*[35] At last, in a cave near Ballymacelligott, about five miles from Tralee, the 14th Earl of Desmond was finally killed, by a band of native Irish settling a private score. His death, however, brought no immediate relief to ravaged Munster. As Spenser described it *"in short space there were none almost left and a most populous and plentiful country suddenly left void of man or beast".*[36] Indeed, even by 1586 the crown victualler reported that Munster was still destitute both of corn, beef, and other victuals for men and horses by reason it remaineth still waste and unpeopled . . ."[37] The defeat and the subsequent attainder of the Earl of Desmond and his

27

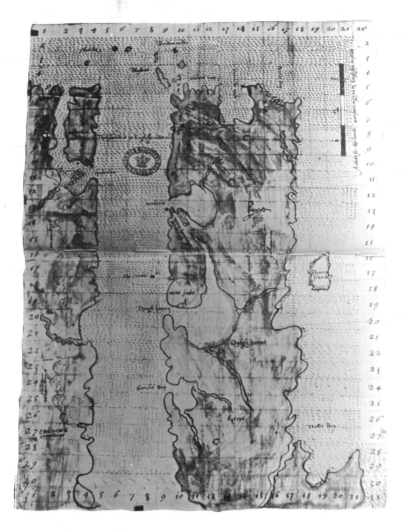

Map of Dingle Bay and Peninsula 1573

associates in 1586, led to the forfeiture of the land of the defeated. It also presented the government with the opportunity for a total reconstruction in Munster; a reconstruction involving a systematic attempt at large-scale plantation, a consistent implementation of English law and customs throughout the province, and the final abolition of the residual powers and privileges of the old lords. Private profit and state security went hand in glove in this reconstruction.

The plantation of Munster and its consequences (which were to be felt right up to the land war of the late 19th and early 20th century) lie outside the scope of this essay. However, a few closing remarks are necessary on the failure of the Hispano-Papal expeditions of 1579-80 to trigger off the great rebellion in Munster which might have seriously challenged the Elizabethan strategy in Ireland. By the late 1570s the great ideological and political conflict between Catholic Europe, whose most powerful champion was Phillip II of Spain, and Protestant England, was moving towards its climax. Within the nation-states of Europe it was not a time for the toleration of religious or political dissent. Religious conformity and national security were seen as inseparable. Religious minorities were a potential fifth column of subversion within the state, and had to be dealt with as such. Thus, for example, the Spanish king had to come to grips with the separatist threat posed by the Dutch Calvinists in the Netherlands. Similarly, in the case of Ireland, the resistance to the Elizabethan conquest had profound implications for the balance of power internationally. In dealing with any threat to the security of the realm Elizabeth's commanders in Ireland gave no quarter, and it was ultimately nothing less than the security of the realm which was at stake in the rebellions of the last quarter of the sixteenth century in Ireland. Yet, as we have seen, the severity and extent of the Elizabethan military conquest was without precedent in Irish warfare, and indeed had parallels only in the experiences of conquest in the new world.' The great Anglo-Spanish rivalry of the late sixteenth century, with its concern for power, prestige and profit, had widespread implications for other more limited but no less vital conflicts. Elizabeth gave consistent 'unofficial' support to the Dutch in their revolt against Spanish control. Those Irish Catholics who, like James Fitzmaurice Fitzgerald, were motivated by the spirit of the counter-reformation, expected similar support from Catholic Europe, most notably from Spain. These expectations were not to be realized during the course of the Desmond wars, when, perhaps the Elizabethan conquest was most open to challenge. Of course, the limited local ambitions and rivalries of the Irish lords, their inability to combine against the common threat of the new system of centralized government, was a major factor in determining the ultimate fate of the

29

Elizabethan conquest. But it would be wrong to ignore the inadequacy of the 'foreign aid' which was available to those in Ireland who were prepared to resist the new order.The Hispano-Papal expeditions of 1579-80 were, both in numbers and in quality, simply inadequate to make a decisive difference to the outcome of the conflict in Munster. In this regard, the ill-starred force which met its horrific fate in the Golden Fort on lonely Árd na Caithne, was but the first entry of a sad litany which runs from the Armada to Del Aguila, from Hoche at Bantry to the lonely **Aud** off the Kerry shore at Easter 1916. Of all of these expeditions it may be said that, so far as their practical assistance to the Irish rebels was concerned, it was almost invariably a case of being too little, too late, in the wrong place or at the wrong time. For none of these expeditions, however, was the price of failure so cruelly dear as it was for the unarmed garrison of Dún an Óir, in bleak November, 1580.

Notes

1. For general background reading the following works are recommended: J. H. Elliott, **Europe Divided, 1559-98**; J. H. Elliott, **The Old World and the New;** D. B. Quinn, **The Elizabethans and the Irish;** Nicholas P. Canny, **The Elizabethan Conquest of Ireland;** D. B. Quinn, **England and the Discovery of America, 1481-1620;** Francis Jennings, **The Invasion of America: Indians, Colonialism¦and the Cant of Conquest;** Nathan Watchel, **The Vision of the Vanquished;** T. W. Moody, F. X. Martin & F. J. Byrne (eds.), **The New History of Ireland,** vol. III, Early Modern Ireland 1534-1691—hereinafter cited as **NHI;** B. Bradshaw, **The Irish Constitutional revolution of the 16th century.**
2. F. M.Jones, 'The Plan of the Golden Fort at Smerwick, 1580', in **The Irish Sword,** vol. 2, p. 41.
3. Seán Ó Faoláin, **The Great O'Neill** (1970 edition), p. 81.
4. See, for example, Sir Charles Petrie, 'The Hispano-Papal landing at Smerwick', in **The Irish Sword,** vol. 9, pp. 82-94; Donncha Ó Conchúir, 'Éirí Amach Ghearaltaigh Dheasmhumhan i gCorca Dhuibhne', in **Céad Bliain** (eag. Mícheál Ó Cíosáin), 1973, pp. 67-87; a useful earlier account is Rev. Denis O'Connor, 'Dún an Óir and the Spanish descent on Kerry, 1579-80' in **Irish Ecclesiastical Record,** vol. XXVI, (1909), pp. 1-18. The definitive assembly and analysis of sources is, of course, Alfred O'Rahilly, **The Massacre at Smerwick, 1580**(1938), a research paper which is exhaustive in combing the relevant sources and which is also passionately argued.
5. Margaret MacCurtain **Tudor and Stuart Ireland** (1972), p. 76.
6. N. P. Canny, op. cit., p. 22.
7. ibid.
8. G. A. Hayes-McCoyin **NHI,** op. cit., p. 91.
9. Perrot's description of the submission, cited Canny, op. cit., p. 148.
10. Petrie article cit., p. 85.
11. Hayes-McCoy believes that eventually the force was 'no more than 700 strong', **NHI,** p. 105.
12. S. Ó Faoláin, **The Great O'Neill** (1970 edition), pp. 77-8.
13. **Calendar of Carew Manuscripts, 1575-1588** (1868), p. 282.
14. ibid., p. 293.
15. Many contemporary accounts describe them as the Biscayaners or 'Los Vizcainos'.
16. **Calendar of State Papers** (Ireland), 1574-85 (1867), p. lxix.
17. At first only three of the ships berthed in Árd na Caithne, to be joined eight days later by the Galleon. On 1 October the remaining two ships had still not turned up at Dún an Óir.
18. O'Connor in **Irish Ecclesiastical Record,** art. cit., p. 1.

19. Petrie, art. cit., p. 90.
20. Cited in O'Connor, **IER,** art. cit., p. 5.
21. Cited in Petrie, art. cit., p. 87.
22. ibid., p. 87.
23. i.e. Hugh O'Neill, for whose early career see Ó Faoláin, op. cit., pp. 1-94.
24. This does not include the women and children.
25. Not to be confused with the seventeenth century saint of the same name.
26. At a place near Árd na Ceártan, according to local tradition; Mícheál Ó Mainín, in **Céad Bliain, op. cit., p. 11.**
27. **Calendar of State Papers (Ireland), 1574–85** (1867), p. lxxii.'28. ibid., p. lxxiii.
29. Cited in O'Rahilly, op. cit., p. 23.'30. Cited in D. Ó Conchúir, art. cit. in **Céad Bliain,** p. 77.
31. See n. 27 above.
32. Cited in O'Rahilly, op. cit., p. 6.
33. Hayes-McCoy, **NHI,** p. 109.
34. **Annála Ríoghachta Éireann,** ed. John O'Donovan, 1851, vol. V, p. 1785.
35. ibid., p. 1793.
36. Cited Ó Faoláin, op. cit., p. 84.
37. ibid., p. 83.

16th Century Stableboy